Friends
Make the
Best Presents

By *Suzanne Siegel Zenkel*

Illustrated by *Patsy Pennington*

PETER PAUPER PRESS, INC.
WHITE PLAINS, NEW YORK

Designed by Arlene Greco

Illustrations copyright © 1999
Patsy Pennington, licensed by
Wild Apple Licensing

Text copyright © 1999
Peter Pauper Press, Inc.
202 Mamaroneck Avenue
White Plains, NY 10601

ISBN 0-88088-390-1
Printed in China
7 6 5

Visit us at www.peterpauper.com

Friends
Make the
Best Presents

You'll have the whole world

in your hands if you

can count a friend

on each finger.

The only plane

on which friendship

can thrive

is an equal plane.

A person can always

be your friend,

even if she is not

a friend in all ways.

Don't just dream of the person you'd like to be. Become that person.

Allow your friend

to make mistakes,

and give yourself

the same freedom.

Accept affection

with open arms,

and give it with

an open heart.

Sow the seeds
of friendship and
your garden will
be forever green.

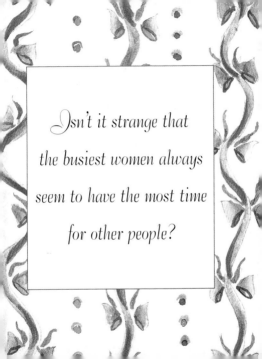

Isn't it strange that

the busiest women always

seem to have the most time

for other people?

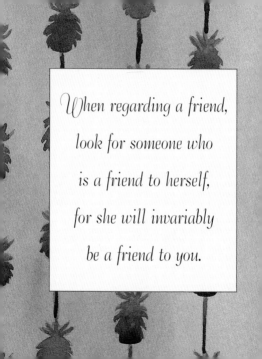

When regarding a friend,

look for someone who

is a friend to herself,

for she will invariably

be a friend to you.

The greatest wonder

of friendship is that

the more you give,

the richer you grow.

A woman's life can be measured not by the amount of wealth she has accumulated, but by the quality and duration of her friendships.

To share your thoughts
with a trusted friend is to
double your happiness and
halve your troubles.

We may dwell
on different shores,
but in the end we are
all in the same boat.

Attitude is everything.

An achievement is so much sweeter when celebrated with a close friend.

Look at things

with a cool head

and a warm heart.

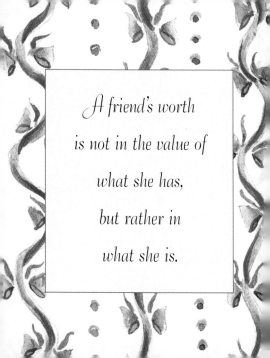

A friend's worth

is not in the value of

what she has,

but rather in

what she is.

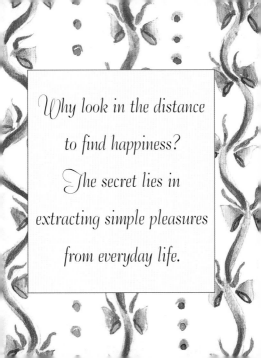

Why look in the distance
to find happiness?
The secret lies in
extracting simple pleasures
from everyday life.

It's awfully nice to have a friend who'll bask in your sunshine—even nicer, though, to have one who'll help you find your way through the darkness.

Your todays will be happier

if you cease to dwell on what

happened yesterday or on

what may come tomorrow.

Of all the world's wonders,

none rises to so heavenly

a plane as that of a true

and lasting friendship.

A friend is like crystal.

Handle with care.

You are twice blessed
if you can travel the journey
of life with a true friend.

Sharing dark thoughts with a friend lightens your heart and turns night to day.

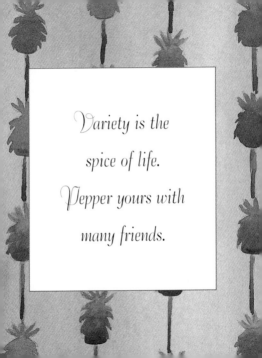

Variety is the

spice of life.

Pepper yours with

many friends.

Be a friend and
you'll have a friend.

Prize your new friends,

and cherish the old.

Sometimes the most valuable thing a friend can lend is a ready ear.

Should you find fault
with a friend, convey it
quietly, but should you have
praise for her, by all means
proclaim it publicly.

Guilt should not be the
motivator of good acts.
Treat others as you
would like to be treated
and your good acts will
flow naturally.

Laughter is a vital force

in life and in friendship.

Seize every opportunity

to have a good laugh.

Pride yourself on being
able to give good advice
to a friend, but even more
in knowing how to accept it.

You can't be

all things to all people

and still be yourself.

A comfortable silence shared by friends speaks volumes.

When your own strength falters, lean on a friend's sympathetic shoulder.

Laughter and compassion
are two vital building blocks
of friendship, but loyalty is
the cement that seals the bond.

Understanding makes

differences disappear.

Don't let anger stand
in the way.
Remember, friendships
need to be nurtured
with forgiveness.

Giving in to

friendly persuasion

can be more satisfying

than getting your

own way.

Friends outlast trends.

Renewing a long-dormant
friendship can be more
enriching than cultivating
a new friend.

True friends delight

in each other's successes

and support each other

in times of sorrow.

Make friends
by being true.
Keep them
by being loyal.

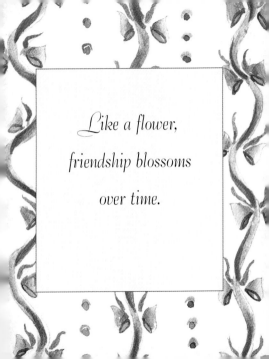

Like a flower,

friendship blossoms

over time.

Don't let the past
discourage you.
Embrace new
opportunities and discover
a rewarding future.

Friends can laugh

at themselves—

and at each other!

Compassion is the

essential link in

the chain of humanity.

There's no more effective cure for loneliness than time spent with a good friend.

Like a good book,

a lasting friendship

has many chapters.

Be yourself.
It's not easy pretending
to be someone else.

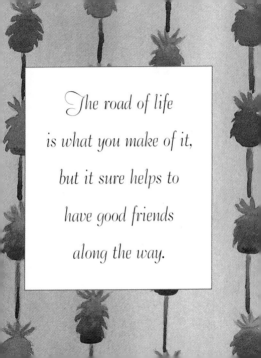

The road of life

is what you make of it,

but it sure helps to

have good friends

along the way.

*A lasting friendship
is marked not so much
by a sprinkling of grand
gestures as by a long
stream of small kindnesses.*

Bury the hatchet
and unearth the joy of
an old friendship.

Be tolerant of your friends.

Even the pick of

the bunch sometimes

has a few blemishes.

To dwell on a friend's

mistake is to make

a second mistake.

Friends are like precious
gems; treasure them
and they will sparkle.

An outstretched hand

is often an invitation

to an open heart.

It is often easier to

reach the mountaintop

if you get an occasional

push from a friend.

Good friends respond

without being called.

Friends drop in when others drop out.

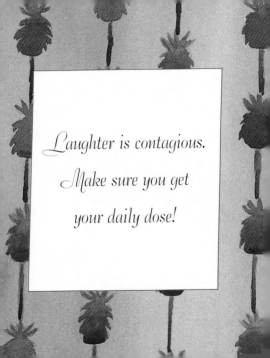

Laughter is contagious.
Make sure you get
your daily dose!

If you open your eyes

and heart to all people,

you will be blessed with

many good friends.

Friendship can endure over many years, even when the content of that friendship changes greatly.